The Killin Branch

A Personal Recollection

Peter Waylett

 Published by Lamplight Publications
260 Colwell Drive
Witney
Oxon OX28 5LW

First Published 2010

ISBN 978 1 899246 23 6

Designed and Typeset by
Lamplight Publications
Printed and bound at
Information Press
Southfield Road
Eynsham
Oxford OX29 4JB

Introduction

Killin nestles on the south west corner of Loch Tay in Perthshire, at the end of the Rivers Dochart and Lochay, which flow into the Loch together at a point just beyond the village.

The River Dochart, a fast flowing river, with the famous 'Falls of Dochart' and the River Lochay, a placid river coming down through Glen Lochay and through a hydro-electric dam.

A pier at lochside used to serve a steam boat service to Kenmore at the other end of the loch. This service ceased in 1939 and was not restarted after the second World War.

The line between Loch Tay and Killin station was closed to passengers on September 1, 1939 except for access to Loch Tay loco steam shed. On November 2, 1964 Killin to Killin Junction closed to freight. A year later on November 1, 1965 the line closed to passengers and a bus service was introduced to link Killin station and Kenmore. The loco shed at Loch Tay closed on September 28, 1965.

The railway ran down to Loch Tay on a falling gradient of 1 : 70 from a junction on the Callander to Oban line and was 5³/₄ miles long. Before it was built Killin was served by a station at Glenoglehead, approximately 4 miles away at the top of Glen Ogle on the Callander - Oban road. It was worked by the Caledonian Railway as a branch of the Callander & Oban Railway.

The branch opened on April 1, 1886 as a rail connection only with no road access.

A single coach provided the branch service with goods run as a mixed train. A school service was provided to Callander. In the last four years a British Railways Standard 2-6-4 tank replaced the ageing Caledonian Railway 0-4-4 tank. On Sundays in the summer during the last years of operation a Six Loch's rail excursion ran from Glasgow and included the Killin branch as far as Killin station. This excursion consisted of a 4-car diesel unit.

Steam operated throughout, until the line closed which was one month previous to the official closure, owing to a rock fall in Glen Ogle.

The section from Dunblane to Crianlarich on the Oban line closed September 28, 1965 also. The last train and stock ran via Crianlarich (Lower).

There was a bus service east of Killin to Kenmore. A bus service still runs to Stirling via Callander on a weekday. A bus service round Loch Tay to Kenmore and Aberfeldy was introduced later.

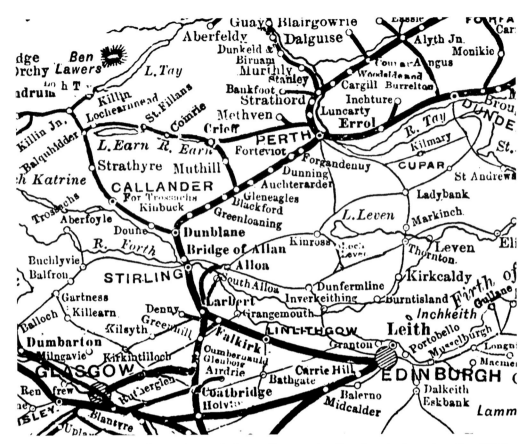

An LNWR map with a view of the railways in Scotland close by the Killin branch from the early part of the twentieth century. Truly remarkable how easy it was then to move around on the various lines to every part.

Photographs in the book are by the author except where stated.

Front cover photograph of Standard 2-6-4 tank no 80093 at Killin station ready to depart for the junction in 1964.

Back of cover a painting by Bill Simpson from a photograph by H C Casserley of the Caledonian Railway tank engine at Loch Tay shed.

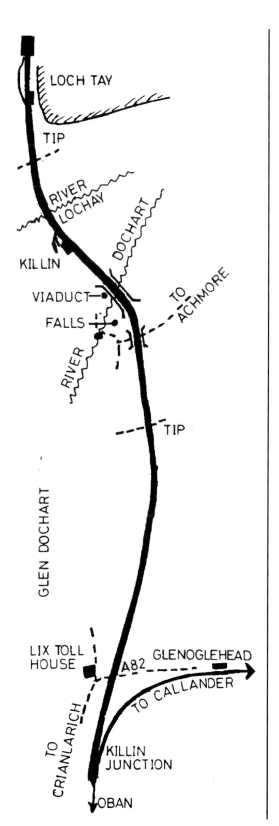

Contents

Map of the
Killin Branch Line

A Branch to Loch Tay

The station buildings on the branch were a simple slopeing roof design with timber frame walls and timber plank infill which gave them a remote frontier look. Although the lamp is a fine robust fixture with its pleasing glow seen from a distance.

H C Casserley

The cheerful footplate crew at Killin station. How could they be otherwise? It must have been one of the pleasantest working diagrams in Britain.

The station at Loch Tay still in service on July 28, 1931 as ex Caledonian tank no 15103 prepares to depart for the junction with the 1.20 pm.train. Distant can be seen the single road engine shed.

H C Casserley

The small 'Caley' tank engine no 15103 pauses at Killin with a train for Killin Junction on July 28, 1931. Truly remarkable to alight from a city journey into this small station amid beautiful highland scenery.

H C Casserley

Unusually with a two-coach train no 15103 approaches Killin with a train from Loch Tay on July 28, 1931. Hard work for the little tank engine working against the severe gradient.

H C Casserley

Early view of the Dugald Drummond engine no 1223 at Killin Junction on June 11, 1927.

H C Casserley

Prominently displayed as an LMS engine 0-4-4T no 15103 1P at Loch Tay on July 28, 1931. This locomotive became the last of the Dugald Drummond class built between 1884 and 1891, it lasted until 1944.

H C Casserley

The engine takes water in the sunlit woodland setting of its shed at Loch Tay on July 28, 1931.

H C Casserley

The mountains give a fine background to ex-Caledonian Railway 0-4-4T no 55173 and its one coach branch train making its way up to the junction, just after leaving Killin station on July 31, 1961. This class of engine was introduced in 1895 by J F McIntosh.

The Caledonian tank in latter years at Killin Junction.

H C Casserley

The junction station on the Stirling to Oban line which up until 1913 was used for interchange with the branch only. Thus the large sign announcing 'Killin Junction change for Killin and Loch Tay'.

H C Casserley

The Callander and Oban line

The Callander and Oban Railway was formed in 1864. After Callander had been reached in 1854 by the Dunblane, Doune and Callander Railway.

Work began to carry the line further into the highlands in 1866 reaching the Killin area in 1870; Tyndrum in 1873; Oban July 1, 1880.

A junction was made near Killin for branch to Loch Tay opened 1877.

The system had a Balluchulish Extension of 27¾ miles opened on August 24, 1903.

All were absorbed and worked by Scottish Central Railways which was in time made a part of the greater Caledonian Railway.

In the grouping of 1923 all Scottish lines were taken over by the London, Midland & Scottish Railway.

Killin Junction

A remarkable exception at the junction on April 19, 1952 with the 6.55 am from Killin in the charge of ex-Caledonian Railway 2F 0-6-0 tender engine no 57450.

H C Casserley

A typical mixed train at Killin Junction on June 6, 1963 in the charge of a Standard 2-6-4T.

H C Casserley

Killin Junction looking towards Crianlarich, with BR Standard class 2-6-4T no 80093 from the branch shunting stock whilst waiting for the train from Oban, which can be seen approaching round the bend on July 28, 1964.

North British type Diesels D6119 and D6109 with train for Oban on June 6, 1963. The Killin branch was on the opposite side to the platform on the left.

H C Casserley

Killin Junction looking towards Callander with BR Standard class 2-6-4T no 80093 waiting for the departure of the train to Callander, before attaching itself to the branch carriage on July 28, 1964. The branch line is to the left of the tall signal box.

Rush hour at Killin Junction on a summer's day in 1962. The departure of the branch train does its best to hide the Callander train in a pall of steam, which is on the right, as it leaves under the raised signal arm.

A view looking down the Glen towards Killin on August 8, 1963 from the early morning train as it descends onto the branch from the junction. The signal box can just be seen to the right of the branch line.

Standard tank 80093 with the 1.52 pm train from Killin to Killin Junction, near Acharn.

H C Casserley

Killin Junction on June 18, 1962, remote and picturesque as a branch line train hopefully collects passengers for its return to Killin. The footbridge was erected in 1913 giving public access to the station

Down — Week Days — **Sundays**

Miles from Larbert		mrn	mrn	mrn mrn only	mrn E	mrn S	aft S	aft	aft E	aft S	aft	aft	aft S	aft E	aft S	aft E		mrn	mrn
	London (Euston) .. dep	..	7 30																	
126	Glasgow (B. St.) ..	..	7 15	10 0	10 10		12 15	..	1 35	1 55	4 0	5 10	7 10	8 0	10 0	10 0	10 0		7 55	..
134	Edinbro (Pr. St.)	..	6 55	9 25	9 25		11 55		..	1 10	..	4 25	5 25	..	9 45	9 45	9 45		..	..
	Larbert .. dep	..	7 50	10 6	10 6		12 50	..	2 9	2 41	4 39	5 44	6 45	8 40	10 42	10 42	11 25		9 57	..
5	Stirling ..	..	8 15	10 58	11 3	12 28	1 7	..	2 33	2 59	4 58	6 1	7 12	..	9 10	10 59	11 0	12 10	9 25	..
11	Bridge of Allan ..	..	8 20	10 53	11 8	12 33	1 12	..	2 38	3 4	5 3	6 6	7 17	..	9 30	11 4	11 4		9 30	..
15	Dunblane ..	..	8 28	11 6	11 16	12 40	1 22	..	2 43	3 12	5 10	6 14	7 25	..	9 30	11 12	11 20	12 18	9 37	..
16	Doune ..	..	8 34	11 12	11 22	12 46	1 29	..	2 53	3 18	5 16	6 20	7 31	..	9 37	11 18	11 26	12 23	9 44	..
24	Callander (below) .. arr	..	8 47	11 25	11 35	1 0	1 41	..	3 1	3 31	5 29	6 32	7 51	..	9 50	11 31	11 43	12 44	10 2	..
	Trossachs H'tel (Mtr) ar	..	..																..	..
37	Balloch Pier (Stmr) ..	..	..																..	..
—	Callander .. dep	..	8 55			1 49		..			6 37		..		12 18	12 13			..	..
28	Strathyre	..	9 12			2 7		..			6 55		..		1 0	10 23			..	..
35	Kingshouse Plat * B	..	9 20			2 18		..			7 10		..						..	..
36	Balquhidder 797	..	9 24			2 16		..			7 10		..			10 33			..	..
48	Killin Junction 749	..	9 46			2 43		..			7 35		..						..	..
47	Luib	..	9 55			2 49		..			7 41		..						..	..
53	Crianlarich 1050	..	10 6			3 0		..			7 52		..		2 25	11 18			..	..
55	Tyndrum	..	10 18			3 13		..			8 4		..			11 33			..	..
70	Dalmally	..	10 42			3 35		..			8 25		..		3 19	11 57			..	..
73	Loch Awe	7 0	10 50			3 43		..			8 33		..		3 38	12 7			..	..
82	Taynuilt	8 17	11 8			4 1		..			8 51		..		4 6	12 27			..	..
85	Ach-na-Cloich	8 25	11 19					..					..						..	..
88	Connel Ferry 158	8 37	11 26			4 15		..			9 5		..		4 32	12 43			..	..
95	Oban .. arr	8 55	11 45			4 25		..			9 25		..		5 5	1 5			..	..

Up — Week Days

Miles		mrn	mrn	aft	aft S	aft	aft	aft		aft	A Calls to set down on notice at Strathyre
	Oban .. dep	..	6 5	..	12 5	..	..	..		4 45	B Sta for Braes of Balquhidder, Loch Voyle, Rob Roy's Grave (about 2 miles)
	Connel Ferry	..	6 21	..	12 22	..	..			5 2	
	Ach-na-Cloich	..	..	..	12 31	..	..	..		5 12	B Central Sta
13	Taynuilt	..	6 35	..	12 37	..	..	..		5 19	C Calls to take up when passengers on platform
22	Loch Awe	..	6 55	..	12 57	..	..			5 39	
24	Dalmally	..	7 2	..	1 4	..	..	..		5 46	E or £ Except Sats
36	Tyndrum	..	7 31	..	1 33	..	..			6 14	F Morning time
41	Crianlarich 1050	..	7 42	..	1 43	..	..	..		6 24	H Waverley Sta
43	Luib	..	7 52	..	1 53	..	..			6 35	P Aft.
51	Killin June 749	..	8 4	..	2 4	..	..	..		6 46	S or S Sats only
59	Balquhidder 797	..	8 20	..	2 20	..	..			7 10	
60	Kingshouse Plat * B	..	8 25	..		..	..	..		7 10	SC Limited 1st and 2nd class. Sleeping accommodation
62	Strathyre	..	8 29	..	2 30	..	..			7 18	
70	Callander (below) .. arr	..	8 46	..	2 47	..	..	..		7 33	$ Will not be detained beyond 12 15 art for connection with 1 0 aft from London (E.) (Larbert dep 11 25 aft)
—	Balloch Pier (Stmr) dp	..	..	..	..	..	..			..	
—	Trossachs H'tel (Mtr)	..	..	..	..	..	..	..		..	X Sat ngt
—	Callander .. dep	7 55	8 50	12 10	1 25	2 55	4 0	5 43		7 36	No luggage or Bicycles will be put out or taken in
78	Doune	8 7	9 2	12 22	1 44	3 7	4 12	5 55		7 48	
82	Dunblane 736 .. arr	8 16	9 11	12 31	1 54	3 16	4 21	6 4		7 57	
84	Bridge of Allan ..	8 22	9 15	12 36	2 1	3 21	4 26	6 9		8 3	
87	Stirling 1032, 1053 ..	8 28	9 22	12 40	2 6	3 27	4 32	6 15		8 9	
95	Larbert 741, 797 ..	8 41	9 41	12 57	2 20	3 44	5 36	6 35		8 29	
123	Edinbro (Pr. St.) arr	9 45	10 45	2 27		4 38	..	7 30		9 50	
117	Glasgow (B. St.) ..	9 15	10 19	1 34	3 8	4 22	6 17	7 10		9 7	
403	London (Euston) ..	..	7 P 5	..	..	..	..			7 F 45	

† Calls on notice at Stirling to set down from Carlisle and South thereof, or on notice to take up passengers for Strathyre and beyond.

LOCAL TRAINS and intermediate Stations between Larbert and Dunblane, page 736.
OTHER TRAINS between Connel Ferry and Oban, 790—Crianlarich and Tyndrum, 1050

CALLANDER, THE TROSSACHS, and BALLOCH PIER.

Miles	**Down**	Week Days	Sun		Miles	**Up**	Week Days	Sun
	Callander (Motor) .. dep	.. ..	.. ..		20½	Balloch Pier (Steamer) .. dep	.. ..	.. ..
10½	Trossachs Hotel (Motor) arr	.. ..	.. ..		20½	Invermaid (Steamer) .. arr	.. ..	.. ..
	Trossachs Pier A (Motor) dep	.. ..	.. ..		25½	Stronachlacher A (Motor) arr	.. ..	.. ..
—	" (Steamer) dep	.. ..	.. ..			" (Steamer) dep	.. ..	.. ..
17½	Stronachlacher A (Motor) dep	.. ..	.. ..		33	Trossachs Pier (Steamer) arr	.. ..	.. ..
22½	Invermaid (Motor) .. arr	.. ..	.. ..			" (Motor) dep	.. ..	.. ..
	" (Steamer) dep	.. ..	.. ..			Trossachs Hotel (Motor) ..	.. ..	.. ..
43½	Balloch Pier (Steamer) .. arr	.. ..	.. ..		43½	Callander (Motor) .. arr	.. ..	.. ..

A Loch Katrine

Bradshaw's timetable for 1909 showing the connections to Killin and Loch Tay.

The Killin Branch Remembered

Killin Junction was a double-platform station with wooden buildings and a footbridge connection to each platform. Branch trains used the Glen Dochart side of the 'up' platform. A brick signal box was situated between the branch and the Oban line on the 'up' side. There was no road connection to the junction station until access was built in 1913.

The line fell away on a gradient of 1:70 continuously down the Glen, passing over the Callander - Crianlarich road near the Lix Toll house on the road junction, and on down under a bridge which led to a refuse tip. Down through the trees and over the road leading to Achmore and the south side of the loch, with the River Dochart and falls below on the left. Still on a falling gradient, and passing above the village and through the trees it reached the fine stone viaduct, which crossed the river, the gradient still in evidence over the viaduct. The line then skirted some houses dropping down to a crossing and reaching Killin Station, approximately 4 miles from the junction.

Killin Station was a wooden building with a sloping roof, and was approached from the village by a short road which ended in a large forecourt. A single platform was provided and a yard branched off at the eastern end. There were no run-round facilities but as the platform was on a gradient it allowed the following procedure. To run round the train at Killin for the return journey the engine would detach from the coach which was effectively braked. It proceeded forward until it could run back through the points into the goods yard siding. The coach would then descend past the point of the siding under control of the guard. With a change of points for the yard siding the engine would run out again to couple up again to the opposite end to haul it back into the station for the return journey.

From Killin to Loch Tay the line was on the level, crossing the second of two rivers on a low steel girder bridge and through the trees, joined by a road which went down to the loch. Passing yet another refuse tip, before reaching the loch side, it ran parallel for the next few hundred yards to the loch side station.

Loch Tay station was another wooden building with sloping roof. There was a single platform and the line ran through to end up in a small engine shed, there was a loop siding accommodating the coal wagon.

The line from the loch side to the viaduct makes a pleasant walk, but beyond has now become part of the countryside. Nothing remains of Killin Junction or Killin Station, on which site has been built toilets and a car park, the yard being used by the Highways Department. The station at Loch Tay is now a private dwelling house and a house has been built on the former site of the engine shed.

The 2-6-4 Standard tanks were introduced on the branch in 1962 and must have provided a muscular advantage with only a single coach to pull! This view of 80126 is in July of that year and is with the engine facing Killin Junction.

H C Casserley

Looking down the line from Killin to Loch Tay from Killin station, the siding is on the left.

H C Casserley

In highland drizzle at Killin station as BR Standard tank no 80093 waits with the 1.42 pm to Killin Junction on June 12, 1962.

H C Casserley

Killin station looking up towards the junction on August 31, 1963. A branch train behind BR Standard class 2-6-4T rests peacefully in the platform after its journey from the junction. Note the liberal number of seats on the platform.

Always the beauty of highlands providing the backdrop to the tiny Killin station in 1964. Note the single diesel unit in the siding

A branch train from Killin to Killin Junction trundles along up the Glen near the Lix Toll House with a single carriage hauled by BR Standard class 2-6-4T in August 1963.

The branch train behind ex-Caledonian Railway 0-4-4T no 55173 enters Killin station after coming down from the junction on July 31, 1961. The viaduct crossing the River Dochart is in the far distance as the line bends to the right out of the picture.

On a warm summer's day ex-Caledonian Railway 0-4-4T no 55173 slowly brings its carriage back up to the platform at Killin station, after collecting it from beyond the siding on July 31, 1961. The carriage had run down from the station by gravity to beyond the siding where the locomotive was waiting to bring it back to the station.

Killin Station with its impressive wooden frontage facing the platform on August 13, 1963. The branch train simmers gently in the platform on its return from the junction. A goods van is seen prominently attached to the rear.

One year after closure Killin Station still stands proud with its rusty track. Compare this picture with the one above. Note the disappearance of the station clock as the real visible change now on September 22, 1966.

Above the swirling waters of the River Dochart BR Standard tank no 80126 crosses the stone viaduct on its way to Killin Junction. The viaduct clearly emphasizes the severe gardient of the branch.

The approach road to Killin station where a train waits to depart for the junction. A single carriage is held in the siding on the left.

H C Casserley

The forecourt of Killin station showing the low wooden structure with its brick out-buildings. The author's car stands outside. Very often the front of small country stations are overlooked by photographers so this provides a valuable viewpoint on July 28, 1964.

The 'Six Lochs' rail excursion from Glasgow crossing the viaduct over the River Dochart after leaving Killin on a summer's day in 1962. These excursions were made up of diesel multiple units.

On occasions, the railway, that had been an incursion in early days provides scenes of comparitive lyrical beauty. This early morning scene is in 1961 as the train crosses the viaduct heading towards the junction hauled by ex-Caledonian Railway tank engine no 55173

Killin Viaduct over the River Dochart which is just beyond the 'Falls of Dochart', a branch train is seen crossing on its way down from the junction hauled by a British Railways Standard class 2-6-4T on a day in August 1963.

A view along the branch from a goods train. The daily goods was once a common and essential feature of branch line railways that became vulnerable to road transport competition.

* for Motor Car Service between Connel Ferry and Benderloch, see page 880.

KILLIN JUNCTION and LOCH TAY.—Caledonian.

Miles	Down.	Week Days.								Miles	Up.	Week Days.					
		mrn	mrn	mrn	aft	aft						mrn	mrn	aft	aft		
	Killin Junc. dep.	8 4	....	9 48	2 50	7 6					Loch Tay §.......dep.	....	9 15	2 20	..		
4	Killin	8 18	8 33	10 3	3	7 20				1	Killin......[861	7 35	9 20	2 25	6 30		
5	Loch Tay § arr.	....	8 37	10 6	3 8					5	Killin Junc. 860 arr.	7 48	9 34	2 39	6 43		

§ Killin Pier, for **Loch Tay Steamers**, see page 934.

The service on the branch advertised in Bradshaw for 1909.

EDINBURGH and GLASGOW to LOCH TAY.—Caledonian and North British.

	Week Days.									Week Days.						
	mrn	mrn								mrn	mrn					
Edinburgh (Princes St.) 849 ...dep.	6 55	1125						Aberfeldy (Coach) ....dep.	....	11 0					
" (Waverley) 849..... "	....	....						Kenmore " ....arr.	....	12 0					
Glasgow (Buchanan St.) 860... "	7 15	12 0						" Pier (Steamer)......dep.	6 50	1215					
Killin Pier .... "	1010	3 10						Fearnan...................	7 5	1230					
Ardeonaig......................	1035	3 35						Ardtalnaig	7 35	1250					
Lawers	1055	3 50						Lawers	7 40	1255					
Ardtalnaig	11 04	0						Ardeonaig....................	8 5	1 15					
Fearnan........................	1120	4 20						Killin Pier 864 ....arr.	9 10	2 15					
Kenmore Pier ....arr.	1210	5 30						Glasgow (Buchanan St.) 861 "	1 0	5 15					
" (Coach)..........dep.	1215							Edinburgh (Waverley) 854 .... "	2 11	6 22					
Aberfeldy (Coach) ....arr.	1 15							" (Princes St.) 854 "	2 17	5 40					

The service beween Edinburgh, Glasgow and Loch Tay.

KILLIN JUNCTION and LOCH TAY.

Miles	Down.	Week Days only.									Miles	Up.	Week Days only.							
			mrn		aft		aft		aft					mrn		aft		aft		aft	
	794 Glasgow (Buch St) dep	..	..	7 15	..	..	12 15	..	5 10	..			Loch Tay ......dep.	..	..	..	..	..	..	..
	794 Edinburgh (P. St.) "	..	..	6 35	..	..	11 55	..	4 25	..	1	Killin ......{arr. dep.	..	..	..	..	..	..	..	..
	794 Oban .... "	6 5	..	..	7 5	..	1 45	..	..	..	5	Killin Junction 794..arr.	7 18	..	9 46	1 51	..	2 38	..	6 43	..
	Killin Junction........dep.	8 12	..	10 6	..	2 6	..	5 55	..	7 45	54	794 Oban	..	1145	..	..	4 35	..	..	..
4	Killin ....{arr. dep.	8 28	..	1012	..	2 15	..	5 2	..	7 55	76½	794 Edinburgh (P. St) "	1045	..	..	4 33	..	..	9 50	..
5	Loch Tay ......arr.	..	..	..	..	..	..	..	..	..	76½	794 Glasgow (Buch St) "	1013	..	..	4 22	..	..	9 7	..

The service in 1942 after the withdrawal of passenger trains between KIllin and Loch Tay

Taking the highlands in their stride the robust Black Five 4-6-0's with two-cylinder climbing power were seen many times in the locality. Here no 45447 is taking the gradient through Glen Ogle with the 12.12 pm from Glasgow to Oban train on July 28, 1954. This is the location where the rock fall blocked the line and caused premature closure of the railway in October 1964.

Loch Tay

A special train at Loch Tay station in the charge of 2-6-4T no 80092 on June 18, 1962.

H C Casserley

Ex-Caledonian Railway 0-4-4T no 55173 returning to its shed at Loch Tay in the evening of August 5, 1961 after a hard days work on the branch.

Loch Tay station on a calm summer's day in 1961, seeming not markedly detriorated considering it closure in 1939. This was due to the fact that it came into private ownership although the railway retained the right to use the line to the locomotive steam shed and watering facilities.

The station building in private hands.

H C Casserley

Loch Tay facing the empty loco shed on July 12, 1957. An ideal subject for space restricted railway modellers.

H C Casserley

The silent and empty steam locomotive shed at the end of the line.

H C Casserley

Rails in the highlands between Killin and Loch Tay in 1961 looking towards Loch Tay.

Passing Lines

Dunblane to Oban via Crianlarich (Lower) serving Killin Junction

Train to Oban near Callander in the Pass of Leny hauled by two Stanier Black Five 4-6-0's in 1954.

Glenoglehead Station after closure of the Callander - Crianlarich section of the line to Oban. It ceased to serve Killin when the branch was built, but the platform, buildings, equipment and loop are still intact on September 22, 1966.

On the original line from Dunblane to Oban via Crianlarich (lower) are two class fives hauling a train from Oban approching Doune in 1954.

Class Five 4-6-0 no 45396 bringing a train to Oban off the Dunblane line from Callander and Stirling at Crianlarich (Lower) whilst a freight train to Oban waits after coming down from Crianlarich (Upper) in 1953.

On the Dunblane to Oban line a train from Oban hauled by a Class Five 4-6-0 approaching the Pass of Leny between Lochearnhead and Callander in 1954.

A bus service was introduced after the closure of the branch line and ran to Aberfeldy via Loch Tay and Kenmore. It is seen here leaving Killin in June 2001.

Presenting the pre-grouping scene with North Brtish engine *Glen Douglas* a Reid 4-4-0 of the North Briitsh Railway at Killin Junction on a railtour in June 1962 organised by the Railway Correspondence & Travel Society and the Stephenson Locomotive Society. Impressive in a distinctive light green with polished brass features presenting an age of proud refinement.

H C Casserley

The engine *Glen Douglas* running light from the Killin Junction signalbox. Note the signal is off on the branch.

H C Casserley

Doune signal box with freight train waiting to proceed towards Dunblane in 1954. The locomotive is an ex-Caledonian Railway 2F 0-6-0 tender engine.

A Ride on the Branch - August 13, 1963

One morning while on holiday in Killin, I decided to take a ride on the railway up to the Junction and back, as the outlook for its survival into the future was not very hopeful.

Leaving the hotel before breakfast, I made my way in the still of the morning up the approach road to the station, the only sound being the twittering of the birds in the trees. On arrival at the station, I purchased a return ticket to the junction for just 2/6 (12$\frac{1}{2}$p) and made my way to the platform. There was a British Railways Standard 2-6-4 tank engine simmering gently in the early morning calm, the driver and fireman leaning out of the cab awaiting departure. Attached to the engine was a single carriage, in which I entered the first compartment and sat down to begin my journey.

With the minimum of fuss, we gently pulled away up the grade towards the viaduct, the carriage groaning under the constant pull of its sturdy charge. We crossed the viaduct with the River Dochart rushing below, its noise drowned by the exhaust of the beat now gathering a steady momentum, over a road bridge and on through the trees with the village far below. Passing the refuse tip, the gulls screaming in competition with the rhythm of the train. Once clear of the trees and climbing out of the glen, the exhaust and clanking of the crank rods echoed back across the hillside. Past the Lix Toll House and over Callander - Crianlarich main road, still climbing steadily. The exhaust beat still strong as the approach to the junction was made. Passing the lofty signal box, standing guard on the left and coming to rest in the side platform without so much as a sigh.

While waiting on the junction platform, the engine uncoupled and busied itself shunting a goods van. It was not long before the train from Oban came rumbling around the bend and into the station. No one alighted, and it departed towards Callander. By this time the branch engine had attached itself to the other end of the carriage and was hissing impatiently to start.

I hurriedly got back on and we were away down the branch, the carriage squeaking and swaying with the motion of the train. The scenery passed much more quickly this time, then all too soon the brakes were applied and the River Dochart and village appeared below. No exhaust beat now, only the constant hissing of steam and the crescendo of the carriage wheels combined with the clanking of the rods and squealing of brakes to be heard. Back over the viaduct and into the station platform with no let-up on the brakes.

I left the station and made my way hurriedly back to the hotel. The village now stirring with life as people were collecting their morning papers from the local shop and guests at the hotel were getting up for breakfast. So ended a memorable ride on the Killin Branch railway, with a record of the journey made on both film and tape for future reference.

One way to ride the line! Modern safety regulators would be appalled. A branch train approaching the crossing near Killin station from the junction in August 1961. The engine is ex-Caledonian Railway '439' class 0-4-4T renumbered 55173 by British Railways.

A mixed train arriving bunker first at Killin.

H C Casserley

From an overbridge leading to a refuse tip near Acharn the ex-Caledonian Railway 0-4-4T no. 55173 pounds its way up the branch towards the junction with a mixed train through the summer landscape in August 1961.

Sketch of a walk from Loch Tay to Killin Junction

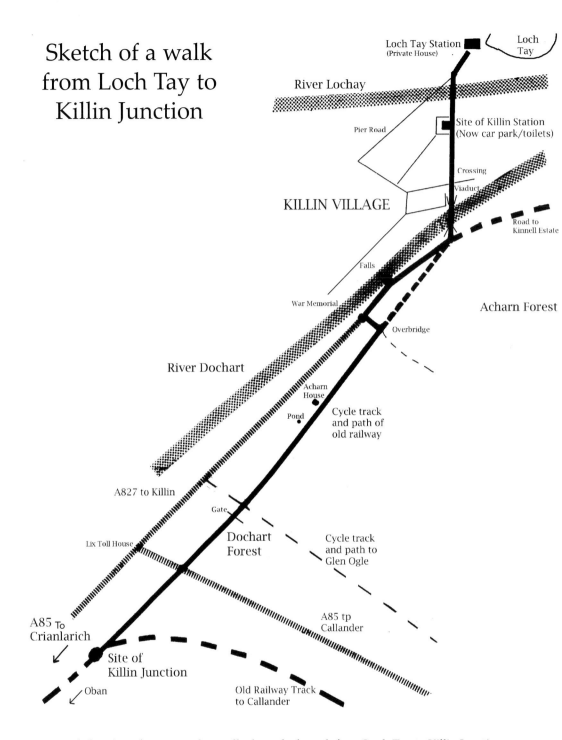

A drawing of a present day walk along the branch from Loch Tay to Killin Junction

A Walk on the trackbed of the closed railway from Loch Tay to Killin Junction in 2006

As Loch Tay station is a private house the walk starts just beyond and goes beside the Loch for a short distance before going through the trees. It follows the pier road for some way, then branches off crossing the River Lochay on a low steel bridge. The track goes behind the back of what was once Killin station, which is now a Highways Department toilets and car park.

Climbing steadily the trackbed reaches what was once a crossing to a house. At this point one leaves the trackbed for a short distance to take to the road. Rejoining it again climbing on an embankment behind the village.

The viaduct over the River Dochart is reached where the parapet is very low and protects walkers with a wire fence. A short distance further a road is reached going to Kinnell estate. The old trackbed carries on through a field with a gate. There is no bridge over the road so one must come off the trackbed and follow the road which comes out by the 'Falls of Dochart', at the west end of the village.

Proceeding along the road out of the village for a few yards one reaches the War Memorial before coming to a public footpath sign for Balquidder, turn left here up a gravel path and through a gate into Acharn Forest, here one must turn right to regain the old trackbed which has now become a cycle track to Glen Ogle.

After going under a bridge and climbing steadily through the trees the road to Killin is viewed down in the Glen on the right side. Continuing and passing, at the time of writing, a pile of sleepers by the side of the trackbed one comes to Acharn House on the right with its pond a little beyond.

The road to Killin below comes out of the trees as one reaches crossroads in the track. The cycle track turns off to the left and continues towards Glen Ogle. Another track on the right comes off the Killin Road. The old trackbed itself carries straight on. It can now be described as a grass track passing through a gate into Dochart Forest. This is a private woodland with public access utilising the trackbed which eventually reaches the main road from Callander to Crianlarich at the junction with the road to Killin at the 'Lix Toll House'.

As the bridge above the road is no longer in place it is necessary to cross the road on foot to regain the trackbed on the other side. Still climbing steadily along the trackbed for about a mile one can see the Oban line trackbed joining at a high level. Upon reaching the site of the junction it is still possible at the time of writing to see a platform face on that side. However the Killin side is completely obliterated and recovered by the force of nature.

The bridge over the River Lochay between Loch Tay and Killin station.

The old track bed over the bridge crossing over the River Lochay between the site of Killin station and Loch Tay in June 2006.

Remains of Killin Junction station in 2006. Only part of one platform edge visible. Also the railway cottages on the right completely gone.

A one time drivers view of the viaduct over the River Dochart four years after closure June 1, 1969. Concrete sleepers are still evident marking the path of the removed rails.

Trees begin to enclose the lonely single line of track after closure.

H C Casserley

Ovebridge crossing the old trackbed between Killin and Acharn looking towards the junction in June 2006.